BUILDING WITH POOP

Jennifer Swanson

Enslow Publishing
101 W. 23rd Street
Suite 240
New York, NY 10011
USA

enslow.com

Words to Know

aromatic Having a distinct smell.

biodegradable Able to be broken down by living organisms or the environment.

brood ball A ball made by dung beetles to house their eggs.

cob house A house made of natural building materials such as dirt, dung, and straw.

concrete A rough building material made of gravel and sand.

flammable Able to catch fire easily.

insulator Something that keeps heat in and cold out.

saliva Watery liquid made in the mouth to help with digestion.

sewage Waste water, poop, and urine.

stucco Fine plaster used on buildings.

Contents

Poop Happens

What is brown and a bit smelly, and you can build with it? It's not dirt or even mud. It's poop! That's right. The stuff you flush down the toilet without any thought could actually be put to good use. Believe it or not, your number two could be a number one building product! Poop is so flexible, it can be molded into pretty much any shape or size needed.

Animals use poop to construct nests, homes, and even fences. People mold poop into bricks for houses and plop it on fences for support. Sound gross? It's not. Poop is biodegradable and

FUN FACT

Poop is normally brown but it can change colors depending on what you eat. Eating more vegetables might make your poop green!

Bird poop provides some of the best and most sought after fertilizer in the world.

environmentally friendly and can make any house more waterproof and aromatic, too. Add a bit of spice to any home construction project!

A Natural Resource

It makes sense to use poop to build things; it's natural and easily found. Building with wood means cutting down trees, which can harm the environment. Building with **concrete** requires a mixer truck, which is not easy to find in some areas. Making a traditional brick out of clay and shale takes time and an oven. Some people don't have access to these materials and tools. So, what do they do? They learn from animals!

Elephants leave really large dung piles. These piles make perfect homes for beetles, scorpions, crickets, and millipedes. They bore deep inside the dung and hollow out their own space.

FUN FACT

The sumac flea beetle uses poop to make its own camouflage shell.

A single elephant can poop up to 300 pounds (136 kilograms) every day! That's 109,500 pounds (49,668 kg) of poop every year.

Ovenbirds and secretary birds use poop from other animals to line their nests. Some animals even use their own poop to hide from predators. The smell is part of what repels predators.

Snug as a Bug in a Poop

Poop pretty much stays where it lands, so it only makes sense that some poop might end up in a nest. Why not? That's how the millipedes feel anyway. Millipedes burrow into the soil to make their nests. Then, they use their own feces to create a protective shell for their eggs. Their feces is recycled bits of decaying leaves and plants, which makes the shells warm and cozy.

Dung beetles also use their poo to house their eggs. They use the waste of animals such as cows and sheep. Some dung beetles will live on top of

FUN FACT

Dung beetles can move dung balls up to 50 times their weight.

Dung beetles use the stars to navigate as they roll their dung balls.

the manure pile. Others burrow deep inside it. Once they find their spot, the dung beetle rolls the dung into a brood ball. The eggs are deposited inside the brood ball. Then the female dung beetle seals up the brood ball with dirt, saliva, and some of her own feces to keep the eggs warm until they hatch.

Tower of Turd

Termites are more than pesky insects who try to eat your house. They are incredible engineers. They build huge towers that you may have seen in images of the savannahs of Africa, with dirt, chewed wood, and yes, their feces.

It makes sense. Termites eat lots of wood. Since you poop what you eat, bits of wood end up in their waste. This makes it quite useful for building. Why? Wood is one of the best building materials on the planet.

The termites push their waste into a pile. It hardens in the sun, creating a solid nest. Some of these termite nests can be up to 30 feet (9 meters)

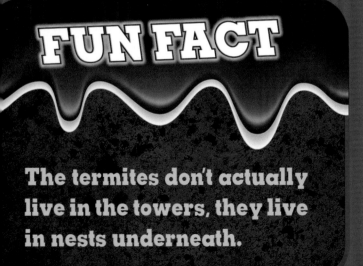

FUN FACT

The termites don't actually live in the towers, they live in nests underneath.

Termites are nocturnal, which means they do most of their tower building at night.

high. They look like big chimneys or vents because they are wide at the bottom and small at the top. How do they get all the poop? Most termite nests house anywhere from 200,000 to 2 million termites. And if they all poop, which they do, that's a lot of feces for building!

Fecal Fences

Animals aren't the only ones who use poop to build. In some rural parts of India, people mix cow dung with mud and plop it on the floors and walls of their houses or on fences. The sticky substance dries and forms a waterproof layer to keep everything dry. It also acts as an **insulator**, to keep the heat in and the cold out. Adding dung is a great way to keep your home warm and dry.

FUN FACT

Elephant dung has lots of fiber, which is great for making paper.

Don't have any cattle nearby? Use elephant dung. That's what they do in Africa. It has the same properties as cow poop and is just as waterproof. Slapping some droppings on a fence will slow the erosion from heavy rains. It's kind

In India, some people paint poop on the walls of their homes to keep them warm or cool, depending on weather.

Wombats have the driest poop of any mammal, which is why it comes out in squares. It's too hard to change shape!

of like using mortar between bricks. When the poo dries, the result is a hard, solid fence that stands for a long time.

Have a wombat nearby? Even better. Wombats actually excrete their poop in squares. Wombats use their cube-shaped poop to mark the edges of their territory. Wombats can't see very well, but their sense of smell is fantastic. By lining their area with their own poop, they can smell when they've reached the end.

Make Your Own Cob House

In remote areas of the world people use dirt, straw, sand, clay, and water to build their houses. These **cob houses** require very little tools to make. Just a bucket or large piece of canvas for stirring, a shovel, and a trowel for applying the plaster.

FUN FACT

Sometimes people press ceramic tiles into the plaster before it dries to make their houses more decorative.

Cob houses, like this one, have poop on their walls for insulation.

Don't have sticks? Use your feet! Simply scoop up a few piles of dirt, add some water, and start mashing. Next, drop in some clay and straw. Now mold it into bricks, about as long as your hand.

Feet make excellent tools for compacting poop into brick shapes. These bricks will dry hard in the sun.

Pile the bricks on top of each other to form a long wall. Push them down slightly so that there are no air holes in between. When it dries, your home will be quite solid.

Want your cob house to last during the rainy season? Slap some poop plaster on the walls. Cow manure might be smelly, but it makes excellent plaster. Stir the cow manure until it is nice and soft and then paint it on with your hands. The poop plaster acts just like stucco that you might find on a house in Florida. These cob houses are eco-friendly and biodegradable. They keep heat in and mosquitos out!

Mixing Manure Bricks

Some communities make bricks with poop! A tile company in Japan is using **sewage** as an ingredient in its bricks. Sewage is the waste-water mix that is flushed down the toilet. When you flush, sewage travels through a maze of pipes

FUN FACT

The average American flushes more than 100 gallons (378 liters) of water down the toilet a day, with their waste, of course.

Sewage is eliminated from water by passing through many different cleaning tanks.

and eventually ends up in a tank at the sewage treatment plant.

There, the water is cleaned and the debris, the waste solids (poop), dirt, and sand settles out.

It falls to the bottom of the gigantic tank, forming a sort of sludge. This sludge is what the Japanese company is using for its bricks.

The sludge is collected from the treatment plant and burned. Poop burns easily since it is full of methane, a gas that is very flammable. What's left over is ash. This ash is mixed with other raw materials like clay and bits of old tile. Then it is molded into brick-like forms and baked.

These bricks are then used to make homes, barns, and outdoor structures. The best part about these eco-friendly bricks is that they allow water to seep through them into the ground. This prevents the builders from having to construct drains beneath the buildings.

Sludge drying beds filter clean water out of sewage through evaporation.

Hold That Flush!

Poop can be used to make many different things: fences, houses, floors, bricks, so why not a toilet? There really is a toilet that does double duty. It captures your number two in a healthy way and is actually made of poop. The Loowatt is a waterless toilet that is made of about 90 percent horse dung.

The Loowatt works like a normal **latrine**, or outdoor toilet. It does not use water to flush away the feces. Instead, it has a unique sealing technology that traps the waste

FUN FACT

While poop never smells great, really stinky poo can signal illness in an animal.

A latrine is an outdoor toilet, usually just a hole in the ground, with some walls for privacy.

inside a biodegradable bag. Unlike a normal plastic bag, this bag will decompose, thanks to animals or the environment.

These Roman toilets didn't even have the luxury of walls, just stone holes.

When a person goes number two in the Loowatt, the waste is captured in this bag and stored. The bags are stored inside a space within the toilet until they are emptied. That could mean a few days or up to a week, depending on how much the toilet is used.

The waste that is collected can then be used for fertilizer, building materials, or even to produce energy. Possibly even another toilet! What a great, biodegradable way to handle feces.

With a toilet made of poop, this thing must be pretty aromatic. Actually, it's not. The special waste bags contain an odor-inhibiting system. It prevents the smell from leaking out and keeps the toilet, and the room where it is located, smelling fresh.

What to Do with Your Doo-Doo

Once you get over the smell, and the weird feeling of handling poop, there are many things you can do with it. Think about it. Poop is completely natural. There is a lot of it around. The supply is limitless, and it's eco-friendly and biodegradable. Why wouldn't you use it to create things?

Wish you could grow plants and flowers like people do in greenhouses? Poop is a natural fertilizer. It contains lots of nutrients that plants and flowers need to grow. Now you can buy a special pot made out of poop. Add soil and your favorite plant and sit back to watch it grow! This pot will fertilize and biodegrade at the same time. What a wonderful way to help the environment.

Ever thought of wearing poop? Try out some coprolite earrings. Coprolite is another name

Plants grow very well in pots made of poop. The pot will fertilize and biodegrade at the same time.

for a piece of fossilized poop. This dried poo is quite a fashion statement. It is used to make many different things such pendants, tie tacks, necklaces, and key chains. What a great gift!

Every day, every animal on the planet poops. That brown or black, soft or hard, a bit smelly

Lumps of coprolite (fossilized poop) may not look pretty, but when formed into jewelry and polished, they can be beautiful.

product is a necessary part of life. Most droppings are left where they, well . . . drop. Humans tend to flush it away. But now, people are learning what animals have always known. Poop is a free construction tool. Why not use some today?

Learn More

Books

Koontz, Robin. *Poop Is Power*. Vero Beach, FL: Rourke Pub Group, 2016.

Lunde, Darrin. *Whose Poop Is That?* Watertown, MA: Charlesbridge, 2017.

Woolf, Alex. *The Science of Poop and Farts: The Smelly Truth About Digestion*. New York, NY: Franklin Watts, 2017.

Woolf, Alex. *You Wouldn't Want to Live Without Poop!* New York, NY: Franklin Watts, 2016.

Websites

Ecology Global Network, "Poop Is Power"
www.ecology.com/2011/10/10/poop-power-biomass-energy/
Read about biomass, material from living things used as fuel.

Kids' Animal Station, "10 Cool Facts About Animal Poop"
kidsanimalstation.com/2012/12/14/10-cool-facts-about-animal-poop/
Learn ten interesting facts about animal poop.

Science News for Students, "Cool Jobs: Delving into Dung"
www.sciencenewsforstudents.org/article/cool-jobs-delving-dung
Read about scientists who study poop.

Index

Published in 2018 by Enslow Publishing, LLC.
101 W. 23rd Street, Suite 240, New York, NY 10011

Copyright © 2018 by Enslow Publishing, LLC.
All rights reserved.

No part of this book may be reproduced by any means
without the written permission of the publisher.

Library of Congress Cataloging-in-Publication Data

Names: Swanson, Jennifer, author.
Title: Building with poop / by Jennifer Swanson
Description: New York, NY : Enslow Publishing 2018. |
Series: The power of poop | Audience: Grades 3–5. | Includes
bibliographical references and index.
Identifiers: LCCN 2017020050 | ISBN 9780766091573
(library bound) | ISBN 9780766091085 (pbk.) | ISBN
9780766091092 (6 pack)
Subjects: LCSH: Defecation—Juvenile literature. | Feces—
Juvenile literature.
Classification: LCC QP159 .S93 2018 | DDC 612.3/6—dc23
LC record available at https://lccn.loc.gov/2017020050

Printed in the United States of America

To Our Readers: We have done our best to make sure all
websites in this book were active and appropriate when we
went to press. However, the author and the publisher have
no control over and assume no liability for the material
available on those websites or on any websites they may link
to. Any comments or suggestions can be sent by email to
customerservice@enslow.com.

Photo Credits: Cover Sam Panthaky/AFP/Getty Images;
p. 2 Vracovska/Shutterstock.com; p. 5 Pilar Olivares/Reuters/
Newscom; p. 7 Anka Agency International/Alamy Stock Photo;
p. 9 Picture Press/J & C Sohns/Getty Images; p. 11 Bjorn
Holland/The Image Bank/Getty Images; p. 13 WIN-Initiative/
The Image Bank/Getty Images; pp. 14–15 Grant Dixon/Lonely
Planet Images/Getty Images; p. 17 Pulsar Images/Alamy
Stock Photo; pp. 18–19 dani3315/Alamy Stock Photo; p. 21
Kekyalyaynen/Shutterstock.com; pp. 22–23 Thomas Imo/
Photothek/Getty Images; p. 25 Wendy Stone/Corbis
Historical/Getty Images; pp. 26–27 DEA/C. Sappa/De
Agostini/Getty Images; p. 29 Fir Mamat/Alamy Stock Photo;
p. 30 Ted Kinsman/Science Source/Getty Images; pp. 31, 32,
back cover (background), interior pages inset boxes (bottom)
jessicahyde/Shutterstock.com; remaining interior pages
(background) Nik Merkulov/Shutterstock.com; interior pages
inset boxes (top) Reamolko/Shutterstock.com.